# Pepper's
# Boredom
# Busters

Ideas to keep
you busy on the
dullest of days

★ American Girl®

Published by American Girl Publishing, Inc.
Copyright © 2011 by American Girl, LLC

Questions or comments? Call 1-800-845-0005,
visit our Web site at **americangirl.com**, or write to Customer Service,
American Girl, 8400 Fairway Place, Middleton, WI 53562.

Printed in China
11 12 13 14 15 16 17 18 LEO 10 9 8 7 6 5 4 3 2 1

Editorial Development: Carrie Anton
Art Direction and Design: Camela Decaire
Production: Sarah Boecher, Tami Kepler,
Jeannette Bailey, Judith Lary
Illustrations: Jenn Ski

## Dear Reader,

Are you bored and can't think of a single exciting thing to do? Then you've come to the right place! Pepper the pup is always on the hunt for fun activities. This book is filled with great ideas for staying entertained when it's raining out, you're on a long car trip, you're hanging out with friends, or you're spending time outside. So turn the page and beat those boredom blues!

## Your friends at American Girl

# Rainy Days

It's raining.
It's pouring.
The whole day's
**NOT**
boring!

# Abracadabra!

While the rain falls outside, stay inside and practice magic tricks to perform for your friends. Here's one to try:

## Pick a Card

Hold a 52-card deck in your hand. Without your audience seeing, take a quick peek at the card on the bottom of the deck. Ask someone to pick a card from the deck and remember what it is. Put the deck facedown on a table. Have the audience member place her card on top and then have her cut the deck. Pick up the deck and fan through the cards, looking for the card that was previously on the bottom. The card to its left is your audience member's card.

# Cookies and Cream

Combine two of your favorite treats for a fun rainy-day snack to make and eat.

## Rainbow Delight

Scoop a little French vanilla ice cream between two colored vanilla wafers. Roll edges in candy sprinkles.

## Graham-tastic

Place a banana slice on a choco-late-covered graham cookie. Scoop a little strawberry ice cream onto the banana slice. Top with another cookie.

# Flip and Find

A scavenger hunt doesn't only have to be something you do outside with friends. You can have your very own scavenger hunt with a stack of old magazines, catalogues, or newspapers and a timer. Below are two lists: one contains words to find and the other includes images to locate. Time yourself as you find things on one list and try to beat that time with the second list.

## Images

| | |
|---|---|
| bird | purse |
| fruit | grass |
| baby | seashell |
| television | flower |
| ring | bicycle |
| puppy | girl in jeans |
| house | cupcake |
| shoe | truck |
| pizza | musical instrument |

## Words

| | | |
|---|---|---|
| purple | word | sister |
| book | ask | back |
| the | more | when |
| simple | fun | happy |
| box | soccer | walk |
| city | ice | read |
| dog | cup | |

7

# Dots & Dashes

Morse code was used to send messages by telegraph. To use it, put a slash / after each letter, and place each word on a new line.

| | | | | | | | |
|---|---|---|---|---|---|---|---|
| A | •— | J | •——— | S | ••• |
| B | —••• | K | —•— | T | — |
| C | —•—• | L | •—•• | U | ••— |
| D | —•• | M | —— | V | •••— |
| E | • | N | —• | W | •—— |
| F | ••—• | O | ——— | X | —••— |
| G | ——• | P | •——• | Y | —•—— |
| H | •••• | Q | ——•— | Z | ——•• |
| I | •• | R | •—• | | |

Decode this message:

•••/••••/•—/•—•/••/—•/——•

\_\_\_ \_\_\_ \_\_\_ \_\_\_ \_\_\_ \_\_\_ \_\_\_

•——/••/—/••••

\_\_\_ \_\_\_ \_\_\_ \_\_\_

•—

\_\_\_

••—•/•—•/••/•/—•/—••

\_\_\_ \_\_\_ \_\_\_ \_\_\_ \_\_\_ \_\_\_

—••/———/••—/—•••/•—••/•/•••

\_\_\_ \_\_\_ \_\_\_ \_\_\_ \_\_\_ \_\_\_ \_\_\_

—•——/———/••—/•—•

\_\_\_ \_\_\_ \_\_\_ \_\_\_

••—•/••—/—•

\_\_\_ \_\_\_ \_\_\_

9

# On the Road

Try these in-car challenges to keep your battery charged on a long trip.

# Suitcase Set

Find the match to Pepper's bag.

# Park Puzzler

This puzzle's like a day at the park—a theme park, that is!
Fit these fun words into the game grid.

admission

attraction

boat

carousel

cotton candy

game

line

outdoor

park

pretzel

prize

ride

roller coaster

show

summer

sunshine

thrill

ticket

water

# The Big What?

## Match these cities with their famous nicknames.

| | |
|---|---|
| The Big Apple | Chicago, Illinois |
| Beantown | Philadelphia, Pennsylvania |
| Crescent City | Denver, Colorado |
| Motown | Detroit, Michigan |
| The Windy City | Nashville, Tennessee |
| Chocolate Capital of the World | Los Angeles, California |
| Music City | Boston, Massachusetts |
| Tinseltown | Hollywood, California |
| City of Brotherly Love | New York, New York |
| City of Angels | Hershey, Pennsylvania |
| Mile-High City | New Orleans, Louisiana |

# Road Closed

Twist and turn your way through this mazy map of detours.

Start

Finish

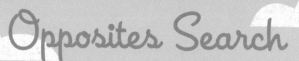

# Opposites Search

It's opposites day! Find each of the words listed below. Listed words can be found up, down, backward, forward, or diagonally. Ready? Set? Stop!

EAST/WEST

NORTH/SOUTH

GREEN LIGHT/RED LIGHT

HOT/COLD

INSIDE/OUTSIDE

FAR/NEAR

FAST/SLOW

HERE/THERE

HIGH/LOW

LONG/SHORT

RIGHT/LEFT

WARM/COOL

```
D  Q  R  R  H  T  S  O  V  G  E  D  L  Q  Q
Z  C  A  T  P  I  S  L  R  O  D  L  T  U  I
S  E  R  Z  H  R  L  E  O  U  I  O  L  T  I
N  O  V  O  I  E  E  W  W  S  C  P  S  Q
N  N  T  G  K  N  R  X  R  S  N  G  N  O  L
Z  V  H  F  L  E  P  E  J  H  I  X  B  H  L
L  T  H  I  E  X  D  L  T  O  L  I  Z  H  M
F  Z  G  T  Y  L  R  I  U  R  O  C  I  A  R
O  H  G  F  A  S  T  O  S  T  W  G  A  O  A
T  H  G  I  L  D  E  R  H  T  H  K  S  W  W
O  N  D  P  N  B  F  I  X  B  U  K  H  K  Y
Q  Y  N  L  H  N  Q  A  P  S  P  O  E  T  V
Y  T  O  F  R  T  O  H  R  C  N  Z  R  W  C
S  O  U  T  H  U  O  F  G  E  O  E  E  R  J
C  V  T  S  A  E  H  O  T  F  J  T  H  E  Q
```

# Who's Missing?

Arrange a big bunch of your stuffed animals while
your friends close their eyes. Once all of the animals are
set up, allow everyone to "study" the arrangement for
15 seconds. Have your friends close their eyes again and
remove one stuffed animal. Have them open their eyes.
The first one to guess which animal is missing wins.

# Theater Time

### What better way to beat boredom than by hosting an afternoon movie marathon?

## Popper Toppers

Popcorn and movies are always a perfect pair. Spice up plain popcorn and let your friends tickle their tastebuds with a variety of microwave popcorn mix-ins.

**Cinnamon Twist**
- $1/4$ cup sugar
- $1/2$ teaspoon cinnamon

**Easy Cheese**
- 2 tablespoons powdered cheese topping

**Tex-Mex**
- 1 teaspoon taco seasoning
- 2 tablespoons powdered cheese topping

Directions: With help from an adult, add one of the above mix-in recipes to a paper bag of microwave popcorn, seal, and shake. Give each girl her own bag to munch on during the movie, and save the leftovers to snack on later.

# Movie Break

Get everyone's energy up
between movies with
a quick game:

## Avalanche!

Don't get buried in
this balancing game.

Collect a bunch of pillows from around the
house. Take turns building a tower of pillows.

The object of the game is to
build the tallest tower without
it tipping over.

If the tower falls, yell "Avalanche!" The
player who builds the tallest tower wins.

# Friendship Challenge

Sit across from a friend. On separate pieces of paper, answer each question about her while she does the same about you. Then compare answers!

## School Stuff

**Easy**
What's your friend's favorite subject in school?

**Medium**
Who was her favorite teacher last year?

**Hard**
What was her favorite project or unit last year?

## Birthday Business

**Easy**
In what month was your friend born?

**Medium**
What is her birth date?

**Hard**
What town was she born in?

## Sports Stumpers

**Easy**
What sport does your friend like to play?

**Medium**
Did she ever play that sport on a team?

**Hard**
What position does she play?

# Animal Answers

### Easy
Does your friend have a pet?
If so, what kind?

### Medium
What's her pet's name?

### Hard
Where did her pet come from?

# Extra Credit

### Hard
Can you list two places your
friend has been on vacation?

### Hard
Has your friend ever had to stay
in the hospital overnight?

### Hard
Can she speak another language?

### Hard
What was your friend's favorite
book or toy when she was three?

### Hard
What does your friend want to
be when she grows up?

# Family Fun

### Easy
How many people are in your
friend's family?

### Medium
Is she the oldest, middle,
youngest, or only child?

### Hard
What are her parents' first names?

# Fashion Funway

Be clothing designers for a day! Make small paper dolls of yourself and your friend, using photos for the faces. Use scrapbook paper, construction paper, and craft embellishments to design all kinds of clothing for the "paper you" to wear.

# Air Ball

It's a race to see which one of your friends has the most hot air. Set up a race track on a flat surface, such as a table or the floor, being sure to mark starting and finish lines. Give each friend a straw and a Ping-Pong ball. Have someone not racing say "go." Without any straw touching a ball, each racer has to blow her ball down the track. The first one to the finish line wins!

# Take It Outside

Sunshine and fresh air
make for a good time
in any season.

# Scream Team

Line up side by side along one end of a big field. On "go," each player yells as loudly as she can while she runs toward the opposite side of the field. Here's the catch—you may run only as long as you can yell! When you run out of breath, stop. See who can go the farthest—and scream the loudest!

# Snowy Maze

Ask a parent's permission to turn your snow-filled backyard into a turning, twisting maze of white. You can start by sketching out a maze map, or just grab a shovel and figure it out as you go. When you're all done, invite your family and friends to wind their way through your twisted winter wonderland.

# Brrr, Bubbles!

If you think blowing bubbles is just for summer days, you're wrong! When it's cold out—really cold!—bundle up in lots of layers, grab some bubble liquid and a wand, and blow away. You just might blow some frozen bubbles that stick around all day.

To make your own homemade bubble liquids, mix together 1 cup dishwashing liquid, $2^1/_2$ cups water, and $^1/_2$ cup light corn syrup.

# Balloon Squirt

Challenge a friend to this tricky race. Mark a starting point in the yard. Each player gets a squirt bottle and a blown-up balloon. The object is to move the balloon to the finish line by squirting the balloon with water. The first player to get her balloon to the finish line wins!

# Water-Balloon Baseball

Here's a fun outdoor activity. Fill several water balloons. Use a plastic bat and have someone pitch a water balloon to you. When you hit it, the balloon will burst! Be sure to pick up the balloon pieces when finished.

# Answers

## Page 13

### Park Puzzler

## Page 14

### The Big What?

Motown = Detroit, MI

Beantown = Boston, MA

Crescent City = New Orleans, LA

The Big Apple = New York, NY

The Windy City = Chicago, IL

Chocolate Capital of the World = Hershey, PA

Music City = Nashville, TN

Tinseltown = Hollywood, CA

City of Brotherly Love = Philadelphia, PA

City of Angels = Los Angeles, CA

Mile-High City = Denver, CO

## Page 15

### Road Closed

## Page 17

### Opposites Search

©/TM 2011 American Girl, LLC